WHISPERS FROM
HEAVEN

WHISPERS FROM HEAVEN

JEANETTE O GRAY

iUniverse, Inc.
Bloomington

Whispers From Heaven

iUniverse books may be ordered through booksellers or by contacting:

iUniverse
1663 Liberty Drive
Bloomington, IN 47403
www.iuniverse.com
1-800-Authors (1-800-288-4677)

ISBN: 978-1-4759-4239-2 (sc)
ISBN: 978-1-4759-4240-8 (ebk)

Printed in the United States of America

iUniverse rev. date: 08/10/2012

CONTENTS

MY LIFE @ 770

I am now seventy years of age. I was born on July 23, 1941.—Jeanette Odom
Parents: James Odom & Bertha Ray.
City Paterson, NJ, 16 Montgomery Street, 8 sisters, 3 brothers.

I learned about God at an early age. And He kept me. I am so grateful.
He gave me 4 wonderful children and 6 grands and 5 great grands. I think
back on a song I know He sweet I know dark clouds may rise and strong
winds may blow but I'll tell the savior he is sweet I know.
Thank you God for everything.

I Love You

My Girls

They are sunshine on a cloudy day.

When it's cold outside they make it feel like the month of May, my girls.

I am so blessed to have such wonderful girls. They make me cry sometimes, but they make me laugh most of the time.

I am so blessed to have them in my life.

There is *Sherry, Sheena, Arlene Marie, Ernestine Susan.*

When I feel down all I need is to hear from one or all of them.

They cheer me up because they have the *juice*, ha, ha!

I am ever grateful to God for being in my life and for giving me such a great gift. My Girls—I Love them so much.

THEY HELP MAKE COMPLETE MAKE DAYS WORTH
STARTING,
PLANNING AND LOVING.
THEY MAKE YOU LAUGH, CRY AND BE PROUD. THEY MAKE
YOU FEEL
LIKE A QUEEN AND A KING.
BECAUSE THEY ARE WRAPPED UP WITH LOVE FROM ABOVE
AND WITHIN.
BECAUSE THEY KNOW IN THEIR LITTLE MINDS AND
HEARTS THEY HAVE
PARENTS WHO LOVE LIFE AND A GOD UP ABOVE, WHO
LOVES THEM AND WILL GIVE LIFE MORE BEAUTIFUL.
IT HURTS YOU TO SEE HOW SOME PEOPLE DOG THEIR LIFE
LIKE LIFE OWES
THEM SOMETHING.
WHEN THIS GIFT WAS BROUGHT WITH SUCH A GREAT
PRICE. LIFE DOESN'T
OWE IS ANYTHING, WE OWE ALL TO LIFE.
WHICH IS JESUS OUR BEGINNING AND SHOULD BE OUR
END.
GOD DON'T MAKE US A PRISONER WITH HIS LOVE.
HE DEMANDS US TO LOVE HIM, WITH ALL OF OUR
HEARTS.
SOUL.
AND MINDS.
WE CAN LOVE EACH OTHER BUT WHEN MAN MAKES
THESE DEMANDS HE
IS SELFISH, HE CAN'T EVEN SEE YOU LOVING OR SERVING
GOD, MUCH LESS
ANOTHER PERSON ON THIS SAME EARTH.
ONLY HIM AND HIM ALONE OR NOTHING OR NO ONE,
THEY WILL EVEN KILL OR THREATEN TO HAVE THIS
INSANE EMOTION
THEY CALL LOVE.

J. CURRY

IF YOU ASK ME WHY I AM GRATEFUL

1. To have a loving Father God

2. Jesus our savior.

3. A loving family—Father, Mother, sisters and brothers, etc.

4. A good husband.

5. Good employees that me and my family.

6. Skills to make things happen.

7. Venture some only read about.

8. God beautiful earth, the change of season, the birds, all the creatures big and small.

9. I am most grateful for the love he put in my heart and mind for others and myself.

Tis so sweet to trust in Jesus.

LIFE, A GIFT FROM GOD

AS I LOOK BACK ON MY LIFE AND NOW LOOKING OVER MY
PRESENT
CONDITION, THIS IS HOW I FOUND LIFE TO BE.
I SEE LIFE AS A GREAT GIFT FROM GOD, SOMETHING TO BE
TREASURED AND
WELL LIVED.
SO OFTEN WE HEAR THIS PHRASE LIFE ROB US, BUT THAT
IS SO UNTRUE
IT IS WE WHO ROB LIFE. ALL THE THINGS THAT MAKE LIFE
WORTH LIVING
IS OURS FOR THE ASKING. MY FATHER GOD SAID TO ASK
ANYTHING IN MY
NAME AND IT SHALL BE GIVEN. ALL WE HAVE TO DO IS
ASK. WHEN I CAME
TO REALIZE THIS I EXTEND MYSELF OUT TO HIM, SEE
BECAUSE I ALWAYS
BELIEVED IN GOD.
I WAS INTRODUCED TO HIM IN MY EARLY AGE. WHEN I
WAS AROUND
FOURTEEN WHEN I GAVE MYSELF TO HIM I DIDN'T SERVE
HIM LIKE I
SHOULD, BUT OH! HOW THE DESIRE WAS THERE SO DEEP
WITHIN, BUT
BEING YOUNG THERE WAS A DISTRACTION IN BETWEEN.
BUT I AM GLAD I FOUND HIM AND HE ACCEPTED ME
BEFORE IT WAS TO
LATE.
GETTING BACK TO LIFE'S GIFT IF WE ACCEPT JESUS
CHRIST INTO OUR
HEARTS WE ARE MAKING A GREAT STEP ALREADY AS
GETTING THE BEST
OUT OF LIFE.

IT IS SUCH A GREAT EXPERIENCE TO BE SAVED.
EVERYTHING IS SO
DIFFERENT, WE HAVE OUR TRIAL AND TRIBULATIONS, BUT
TO SUFFER AND
KNOW JESUS MAKE IT SO BEAUTIFUL, HE PROMISED
NEVER TO LEAVE US.
AND THAT THE LEAST WE CAN DO TO PAY FOR SUCH A
GREAT GIFT IS TO
CARE FOR ONE ANOTHER.
WHEN IT BECAME HARD TO PRAY THINK BACK ON THE
CROSS. AND WHEN WE THINK ON THE WORD **LIFE** THIS
WORD SHOULD COME TO MINE **LOVE**.
GOD SO LOVED THE WORLD, HE GAVE OF HIS ONLY
BEGOTTEN SON, THAT
LOVE.
WE SHOULD BE ABLE TO GIVE GREAT GIFTS TO GOD AND
OTHERS AROUND
US.
I HAVE SUCH A LOVE FOR LIFE THAT ALL I CAN DO BUT
PUT MY SELF IN ITS
WAY TO BE USED AND TO LOVE.

I LOVE GOD WITH ALL MY HEART AND MIND. THAT HE
ASKS OF EACH WHO
PICK UP THE CROSS.
AND THEN THERE'S A MAN IN MY LIFE WHO HELPS ME
MAKE MEANING.
HE HELPED BRING ME BACK TO GOD SEE HE WAS PRAYING
WHEN I WASN'T.
HE KNEW ABOUT LIFE AND ABOUT IT'S GIFT AND HE
CARES ENOUGH TO
SEEK THIS GIFT FOR ME.
AND I LOVE HIM FOR BEING WHAT HE IS, NOT ALWAYS
WHAT I WANT BUT

BEING HUMBLE ENOUGH BE STILL BUT THE FATHER WHO
MOLDS US ALL,
WHO LOVES AND FOLLOW AFTER HIM. THIS LOVE I SPEAK
OF BRING ONE
THING BACK TO MY MIND. MY FAVORITE POEM

FEBRUARY 2011

Feb. 21st: This is the first day I have set at my desk attempting to write.

Blessings

G is for *Blessing* only God can give.
O is for *faith* that we must have to receive your blessing
D is for *gratefulness* we must be for all our Blessing
God so loved the world he gave his only son so we may seek and request our Blessing
So to *sum* it all up "GOD"

Blessings

I AM SO GRATEFUL

I've been so blessed.

When I look back over my life I can see plain as day they never thing we went through. But God never left me alone.

As a child I learned that he would never leave us alone. And you could count on his promise. I look to Him and He blessed me.

God taught me you don't have to be rich to live well you just have to have Him in your heart and mind and do His *will*. I love to sing Oh!

Now I Love Jesus *because he first Loved me*. I was already blessed before I knew Him because He knew me first and loved me.

Faith 4/7/11

Oh!! How I Love Jesus because he first loved me
What a gift one that shouldn't be tossed aside
Because he is always there for me. I can't stop talking about Him. He is *real*, trust him, tell him your needs and wants he knows before you ask but we must be humble and ask.

I Love the Father and the Son, Holy Spirit
You can't make me doubt Him
I know too much about Him
He loved me before I knew him a real Father
All this gave me the faith put all things in his hand
There is a song I love to sing, I love sing it's worth it sound like music to my ears. Oh how I love Jesus.

Thank you God for all your beauty and wonders and love.
Thank you Lord

J.O.G.

I Think I am
Going To Testify

I first heard about the wonders of God when I was a toddler. My mother would read out of the Bible the birth of Christ. The Christmas story.

Then when I was older we went to church and one day God sent a godly woman into our neighborhood and she would have all the kids that wanted to know about God.

And she taught us a song that gets me so excited and goes like this: Oh! How I Love Jesus, and it means so much to me. Why you ask, because he first *Loved Me*. Just like a parent we love our children before we even see them. Just think God so loved the world that he gave only Son to save a sinner like me. And I am so glad that Jesus lifted me and saved my soul. I might lived like I should always but I stopped and listen so I go back to God with clean hands and a pure heart. Thank you Jesus. God is so good to me I can't stop talking about Him.

God is so real you can't make me doubt Him.

Just waking up is a blessing. And looking at all the wonderments and I know only God never be taking for granted.

I look up and know only *God* He is wonderful I love Him so much.

I never said I wouldn't tell anyone about God.

I can't help but tell everyone and anyone who would listen about the goodness and wonders of God, it's all around. Let go and let God He loves you also give and in return He will give you. Thank you God I Love you so very much.

Jeanette

God—Father, God + Man

There is no Greater Father than Father God.

If men would take example of our Father God. We would have a lot of good men.

Where does it say in the Bible that men had to be hard and strict where there is no reasoning.

God is a *parent*, loving, forgiving, not unreasonable, abusive or uncaring. God takes care of all our needs, he is forgiving, caring, he never leaves us alone. He never makes someone or something more important than His children. I am so glad He first loved me and been around to raise me these 69 years never leaving me alone. Answer my cries, showing me right from wrong. He gave us rules to live by that life can be good. He gave his only son that all the rest of His children can have a better life.

Women Misused and Abused

As a child I grew up seeing men abusing women, the ones they said they *love*.

Back then I couldn't get away from the crudent. Seem like every home had this going on.

I thought it was alcohol and arguments.

I had told myself I would never marry a man who drank and I would not argue.

But I fell for someone who didn't drink, a con man, a preacher. I didn't have to talk back or argue he was just a bully.

I was glad I left before one of my children got killed or myself.

Only good thing that came out of being with him was my girls, my joy.

WHAT IS LOVE BASED ON?

I found love to be based on many misgivings.
I found it to be very one side.
You give and other person just takes without giving anything in return.
It has been like that all my life.
My life is a stepping stone for another
person to climb or grow.
And when they reach their goal I am just cast aside with
a broken heart and emptiness.
There goes my reason for living.
I based my love on hope and dreams.
I based my love on feelings one for another, the
love God speaks of "Love ye one another, do not do onto
others as we would not have them to do us,
Trust, Sharing and Understanding."
I find these are for story book children.
Love does not exist it is a thing of the past.
I just came a long a little too late.
I am not feeling sorry for me.
I am just stating facts and feeling sorry for
those who never experience love and loving another.
My love I feel for others makes me a better person.
It makes me happy it makes me worth living.
So often I gave it and the feeling of what
I have received only made me want to die.
Old death was not ready for me,
so I keep slipping in and out of love.
Unfortunately, love is never returned to me
it is abused, misused and refused . . .

EMPTY VESSEL

Today as I sit with this pen in my hand with no thoughts or dreams.
I feel like an empty vessel with nothing to give and receiving the same
"nothing."
No special person or thing in mind to make me feel full until I over flow
with Love and Joy and
Peace and Happiness.
I have once known life today to seem so meaningless it doesn't even seem
worth living.
But I live on to empty to die for, if I was full with sickness there would
be a chance of dying.
But no I am healthy as can be with no aims or direction to go.
I am not only empty but kind of broken up too, with no mending power
and to weak in mind to
look up and call on you "Father God" to look down on this vessel and
mind it and than to fill
it until it over flows with love and life and all the things that make each
day worth getting out of
bed for.
I look at a pitcher I own it's beautiful, it's art glass with no flaws and
with nothing in it it's
full funny but you see the person who gave it to me is full of love for
God and for her fellow man
and life, so I feel it is full.
Here I am a person who at one time was so full of Love and Life and for
everything around me.
I felt like a beautiful vessel so perfectly put together, so happy just
looking around and looking
upon my children and my husband and to take care of them and love
them was everything I
wanted to do each and every day.

But God you played the biggest and best part in my life the day I found
you were real in my
soul.
And then you surround me with so many beautiful people who sang
praise in your name and
played such prayers of faith, these are things which kept me full each and
every day and now I
lost all and I don't know how or if I will ever make it back where I may
be a useful vessel.
I feel if I ever find love again for this is what I need so very much, for
when I am in love so
may other beautiful things happen to me.
Who God? Who! will mend this broken vessel than fill it until it over
flows . . .

THE IMPOSSIBLE DREAM

I Had a dream of one day possessing all the beautiful things that life
have to offer.
Starting with me to be beautiful, a dream walking.
Than to be supply with whatever it takes to supply a dream clothes,
jewelry, car, money and a beautiful home.
A man whom can possess my soul my mind, all of me.
Because all he could see was me, a love that would never die. To shower
me with riches of this earth.
To make me laugh when I was in the deepest pit.
To make me cry just to think that one person can be so loved by another.
What ear of joy to know it is.
I whom capture his heart and mind and made him captain of my soul.
In my small mind I hold a Dream some day he will come along the man
I love.
But to now I hold close in my Impossible Dream.
But you see I already met the Man many years ago.
He has given so very much of himself even thou it does not show.
He made me rich with treasures the world can never take, of heaven
dream
and promises that still exist even when I was awake.
If you look upon me, you would see i am not Beautiful, I am not rich
with the things of the world.
But I have the man who captured my soul and he has given much more
than money
can buy, he has given love, his kids to share my dream.
We have our love and we have each other it may not seem like much,
after all I said I like.

But in the shape the world is in today we are rich because love is hard to find.
In times like these it makes you wonder what dreams are built on today no love not even a dream.
I can't help but to want to cry when I look at my riches, my jewels and my captain.
Then I realize It's no longer a dream but a reality of
"My Impossible Dream."

THE HISTORIAN

I Feel like a historian who has been through the mill with so many stories,
I can hardly sit still.
About love affairs and broken hearts and disappointments to.
I don't know where to begin or is this because I'm through.
Because these are things which happen in the past and we all know it's true.
It happen to our ancestors and its happening to me and you.
The future is a unknown stat that only fate may know.
But this is something no man can ever say is that "I told you so".
For the future is not for us to say, for all we can do is plan and pray.
Until old fate happen along our way to tell us to stay or go.
I know I may not be famous.
I know I may not be known.
But I know I have made history because I have a heart of stone.
Wise men say that fools wish in where angels fear to tread.
So I guess that is why we fine so many dead.
Too many used their hearts instead of using their head.
I have traveled that route but it left me wounded, can't you see?

CHILDREN OF TODAY
—1970 TO 2011

First God →
It is said to *honor* thy mother and father and your day will be long.

They seem to have no time for God or His word.
I guess if he would text them maybe or maybe not.
Sex, text and drugs and game
Give them a game or a phone a whip and a gun.
So mom and dad knows who Boss
They show no respect because you owe them they didn't ask to be born. How can they be so wrong.
You love them and protect them then you need to get protection from them. That is because they don't fear God, the father, the *father* and the parent of us all. Trust this the punishment is more severe than they can ever know and no one to protect them from it trust this.
Honor thy father and mother said Father of us all
God

TO MY HUSBAND

THIRTY YEARS OF LOVE THE FIRST DAY I SAW YOUR
FACE, I DIDN'T REALIZE WHAT WAS TAKING PLACE. A
UNION OF TWO LIVES THAT MULTIPLE INTO FOUR.
NOTING SO INCREDIBLE HAS HAPPEN TO BE BEFORE. I
LOVED YOU THAN. I LOVE NOW AND SOMETIMES EVEN
MORE. I KNOW WE HAD OUR UPS AND DOWN. AND
SOMETIMES
IT SEEM LIKE WAR. MANY BATTLES. NEVER KEEPING
SCORE. OUR LOVE HAS OUT LASTED AND OPEN MANY
DOORS. OUR CHILDREN WAS OUR PRIZE THAT GREW
BEFORE
OUR EYES. AND TIME MARCHED ON BEFORE WE REALIZED.
WE SCORE A PERFECT SCORE THIRTY YEARS AND I EVEN
LOVE YOU MORE.

HAPPY ANNIVERSARY

THE RAPE OF
THE BLACK MAN

Oh! What fools we are to believe we are to illiterate and couldn't be taught or to think intelligently TRICKED into darkness with our eyes wide open. Taking advantage of used and abused, made to work from sun up until sun down to service others in every way possible with our bodies and our minds and not being able to refuse, raped in every way imaginable, men STRONG Black Men.

We stand in the light of time and nothing changes we are still being raped and sodomy with no defense, with the justice system turning its head. Why have we given up, lost our faith sunk so low, because no one hears our cry, no one sees the blood spilling into our streets, no one feels our wounds. SO We throw up our legs and open our arms and embrace the rapist trying to ease the pain. The result of these rapes ends also in pain and hurt a lot more than the victim, it hurts his loved ones and all those like him. Because there seems to be no better tomorrow and the disease keeps spreading.

Oh! What a crime this is. Oh! What a loss. "BLACK MEN, STRONG BLACK MEN RAPED."

July 17, 1996
J. Curry

BEAUTIFUL PEOPLE

The world has a saying, beauty is only skin deep. But I said it goes
farther than that.
The real beauty comes from within a body; it comes from the soul and
the heart.
It is a state of mind, it comes from God, and he made us beautiful
because he made us his own image.
And my God is beautiful, everything he made is good, he said so himself.
You cannot make me doubt him because today I can truly say I know
too much about him.
I always consider him a great artist just looking at his work in nature.
But now since I give myself to him, he shows me everything is beautiful
in its own way.
He gave man this beauty and left him with the decision to let it shine,
that the world may see it.

I am so glad I yield myself to Father God and let him guide me to where
ever he may.
I love the way he has lead me to all the paths and journeys, for I know
no cross, no crown.
I found him to be just what he said he would if we let him come into
our hearts.
In my daily walk through life with God I meet so many beautiful
people . . .

Your Child My Friend

I know you lost your baby not so long ago
You know you will see her even though
Time goes by so slow

She have not left you lonely, a vacation
She was in need of. Thing of this world
Are sometimes harder than we can bear.
So God sometimes steps in and He takes us
From this earthly home to heaven for some
Rest, because He knows our work on earth
Will take us to our death.
We know how she was a blessing to all the lives she touched
Even though she was just a baby
She gave the world so much.

IT'S A CRIME WHAT'S ON YOUR MIND
SO STOP LISTEN TO YOUR HEART AND WHAT
YOU'RE THINKING BECAUSE IT'S REAL! YOU WILL GO TO
JAIL WITH NO BAIL IT'S ALL REAL. YOU DO THE CRIME YOU
DO THE TIME. BIG BROTHER IS WATCHING YOU>>JUST A
REMINDER! WORK NOT FOR
JERKS SO BECAME A CLERK AND STAY ALERT! DON'T GET
CAUGHT UP IN SOMETHING YOU THOUGHT UP BECAUSE
IT'S WRONG, YOU MUST BE STRONG.
IF YOU WANT TO SAVE AND BUY A RIDE GET A JOB. DON'T
STEAL KEEP IT REAL OR YOU WILL GO TO JAIL.
SO STOP LISTEN TO YOUR HEART AND WHAT YOU'RE
THINKING. DON'T GET TAUGHT UP OR THE NOISE YOU
HEAR WILL BE CELL DOORS CLINGING.

JEANETTE CURRY

OH! HOW I LOVE THEE I CAN NOT BEGIN TO COUNT THE
WAYS.
THERE ARE SOME LITTLE GIRLS IN MY LOVE LIFE TO AND
THEY RANGE
FROM AGE 6 THRU 11.

THE REWARD OF
BEING A MOTHER

I myself, am the mother of four lovely daughters. They were a joy to me from the very beginning of their lives. I had so much pleasure watching them grow into little people, learning to "make sounds and smile," seeing the changes rolling over, sitting up and holding on trying to walk. I began saying to myself "Here comes the real fun, catch me if you."

And oh boy! trying to understand what they were saying was another test. I wouldn't have wanted to miss any of it for truly it was special. Son, they could *talk* and *walk*, then *run* and *drive*.

Then difficult changes began and I felt maybe I should not have children was I doing a good job as a parent. We mothers doubt ourselves. All we can do is pray and ask *God* for *guidance*. With all these changes we make it thorough and the rewards are great. The children become wonderful adults, good friends and good citizens.

THE REWARDS OF BEING A MOTHER: I MYSELF AM A MOTHER OF FOUR LOVELY DAUGHTERS. THERE WERE A JOY TO ME FROM THE VERY BEGIN OF THEIR LIVES. I HAD SO, MUCH PLEASURE WATCHING THEM GROW INTO LITTLE PEOPLE, LEARNING TO MAKE SOUNDS AND SMILE. SEEING THE CHANGES. ROLLING OVER, SITTING UP AND HOLDING ON TRYING TO WALK. I BEGIN SAYING TO MYSELF "HERE COMES THE REAL FUN CATCH ME IF YOU CAN" AND OH BOY! TRYING TO UNDERSTAND WHAT THEY WERE SAYING WAS ANOTHER TEST. I WOULDN'T HAVE WANTED TO MISS ANY OF IT FOR IT WAS TRULY SPECIAL. SOON THEY COULD TALK AND WALK, THEN RUN AND DRIVE. THEN DIFFICULT CHANGES BEGAN AND I FELT MAYBE I SHOULD NOT HAD CHILDREN WAS, I DOING A GOOD JOB AS A PARENT. WE MOTHER DOUBT OURSELVES. ALL WE CAN DO IS PRAY AND ASK GOD FOR GUIDANCE WITH ALL THESE CHANGES WE MAKE IT THROUGH THE REWARDS ARE GREAT. THE CHILDREN BECOME WONDERFUL ADULTS. GOOD FRIENDS AND GOOD CITIZENS. AND WITH LUCK AND GOD BLESSINGS WE BECOME GRANDPARENTS TO MY GIRLS: SHERRY, SHEENA, ARLENE AND SUSAN—LOVE

MOM

Subj: PRINCE KEYON
Date: 6/11/2010
To: *nicolekeyon2171@msn.com*

MY NAME IS KEYON. SAY THAT? NOT LEON, KEYON WITH A.K. I JUST ARRIVED TODAY. I AM MY DADDY BABY AND HE SO PROUD. HE WAITED SO PATIENT JUST FOR ME. AND HERE I AM BORN TO BE FREE FOR THE WORLD TO SEE JUST LITTLE ME. WHEN I LOOK IN MY MOM EYES I CAN SEE LOVE ME. AND I WAS MEANT TO BE A LITTLE BOY WITH A GREAT HEART AND LOTS OF LOVE FOR THEE. IF YOU MET MY DAD YOU ALREADY KNOW ME. BECAUSE HE'S A MAN I LIKE TO BE. I WOULD LIKE TO THANK GOD FOR US THREE. ME AND MY WHOLE FAMILY.

LOVE GRANDMA JEANETTE

Friday, June 11, 2010 AOL: Jeanetteogray

DON'T BREAK
YOUR MOTHERS

FROM THE TIME OF BIRTH ON THIS EARTH SHE LOVED YOU.

SHE WAS SO PROUD TO SAY OUT LOUD THIS IS MY SON, HE'S A GOOD ONE, HE'S A STRONG ONE AND A SMART ONE. WITH LOVE IN HER HEART A SMILE ON HER FACE SOMETHING ONLY YOU CAN REPLACE WITH SADNESS AND SORROW AND DISGRACE. I TOLD YOU SHOW YOU RIGHT FROM WRONG. I LEAD YOU I FEEL YOU. I TAUGHT YOU, I BROUGHT YOU. WHY DID YOU GO WRONG? DID YOU NOT LOVE ME ALL ALONG? WAS I WRONG, WAS I NOT STRONG? YOU WERE SUCH A BEAUTIFUL BABY THE BOY OF MY DREAMS. THE SMILE ON MY FACE YOU ERASED. MY HEART FULL OF JOY YOU EMPTY IT INTO PAIN . . . WAS I SO BLIND OR WERE YOU SO VAIN. YOU BROKE IT MY HEART AND I GAVE YOU SUCH A GOOD START.

JEANETTE CURRY   7/23/2004

JESUS AND ADVI

The day I met Advi I knew she was a gift
Tiny as she was she gave the world a great, big gift
We as parents love her and her great big kiss
The talent that she has, it is something that can't be missed
Jesus loves her, yes, I know
Because the bible tells us so.

Advi can sing, draw and dance
I believe that she can bless us all
Oh, how I love Jesus because He first love me/ her/ us all

SLIDE FOX

Once upon a time, there were three hot chicks, Red Ridinghood, Goldilocks, and Cinderella. One day, they were all talking about a cute guy. But they didn't know his name so they went to the place where they heard he hang, at the farm.

So off the three went looking for the farm where he hung out.

They all walked in and there he was, swagging over to Little Miss Muffet.

And they walked until he was close to her, and they rush him saying, "Don't believe a word he's saying because he is a fox. A Slide Fox who can't be trusted."

And he turn around and couldn't believe his eyes; all of the women he tried to fool.

But this time, he knew his Goose was cooked.

Amen

62nd Birthday

TIME

THERE'S TIMES IN OUR LIVES
WE SHOULD ALL BE TOLD
HOW SPECIAL WE ARE
AND HOW MUCH WE ARE LOVED.
JAKE, TIME HAS COME TO THE KINDEST,
HARDEST WORKING MAN
I HAVE EVER KNOWN.
JAKE, MY CHILDREN AND I
WANT TO SAY *THANK-YOU*
FOR YOUR LOVE AND KINDNESS.
SO TONIGHT IS YOUR NIGHT.
WE WANT TO GIVE
YOU BACK SOME OF
THE HAPPINESS
YOU HAVE GIVEN US.

TIME

Time passes so slowly as if it is unconcerned.
The minutes, seconds and hours oh, how my heart burns but it's when
I'm with
you that it feels like good wine. The kind we would devour in just a little
time.
The times we spent together were so precious and so sweet.
It makes time so unbarring until the next that we shall meet.
If I was to possess the power to halt the hands of time.
I'd put in my pocket and have all behind.
The minutes and the hours would be what it would be a servant to my
feeling
and the things that divine me.
I don't possess the powers to halt the hands of time.
For I'm just another stranger passing in the night and being overcome by
time.
It is just a losing fight, for time would be the winner for that the
way it's planned to leave it in the hands of God, not
in the hands of man.

AS I PASS THIS WAY

AS THE 21ST CENTURY CLOSE I AM STILL ALONE. WAITING FOR LOVE TO FIND A HOME. A HOME IN MY HEART AND MY LIFE. I NEVER THOUGHT I LOVE SO LONG AND BE SO ALONE WITH NO MAGIC. NO LAUGHTER NO WARMTH. I SUFFER IN SILENCE WITH A BROKEN HEART. IF EVER I SHOULD PASS IN THIS COLD INDIFFERENT WORLD, I CERTAINLY WOULDN'T LAST AS LONG. FOR YOU SEE THIS OLD HEART OF MINE IS MADE OF GLASS. IT BEEN BUMP AND DUMP STEP ON BROKEN TOTALLY IN HALF

RESTAURANT

7/20/2008   SUNDAY

              THE RESTAURANT

LAST NIGHT I WENT TO a restaurant called MUSIC. THE CHEFS WERE SERVING FOOD FOR THE SOUL. IT WAS WONDERFUL AND FILLING, IT FILL THE MIND, THE HEART, AND THE SOUL. THE FOOD WAS SERVED IN JESUS NAME. THE MAIN MEAL WAS THE DIXIE HUMMING BIRDS. SO REFRESHING THE FLAVOR WAS A HIT WITH EVERYONE THEY LOVED IT. THE PRICE WAS RIGHT ALL YOU HAD TO PAY WAS A OPEN HEART AND MINE IN JESUS NAME. THEY SERVED A OLD RECIPE ONE THAT WAS GOOD FOR MY DEAR MOTHER AND THOSE WHO BELIEVED OR WAS RAISED ON SUCH FOOD. A MEAL LIKE THIS IS ENJOYED ALL AROUND THE WORLD AND REFUSED BY NONE. THIS FOOD IS GOOD TO EVERY RACE OF PEOPLE ALL AROUND THE WORLD THAT OLD TIME RELIGION GOOD STUFF PRAISE GOD.

FROM THIS DAY FORTH

From this day forth,
I will tell the world that I will take you as my wife.

I will do this for life.

I will give you my all and always stand tall, because you
are the love of my life.

From this day forth, I am your man

Count on me, you always can.

Your husband, your biggest fan.

I love you today and this day forth.

LOVE

LOVE IS SO ILLOSUSE IT FASTER THAN THE WIND. YOU'RE IN AND OUT BEFORE IT BEGEN. I TRIED TO HOLD IT TIGHT IN MY HAND BECAUSE WHEN I PUT IN MY HEART THAT WHEN IT RUNS. THEN I COME TO REALIZE I AM NOT THE ONLY ONE SEARCHING FOR THIS ILLESION ONE THE ONE WE CALL THE WIND/BUT THE ONE WE KNOW AS LOVE

Address 1 Address 2 Address 3 Phone Email

The Turn Around Kids

4/22/12

I have 2 daughters that were headed in the wrong direction and God step in and gave them another go at life. The drugs was stop and just when they wasn't sure of what was next he gave them a purpose in life that is so wonderful and rewarding. I am so proud and happy that their way was not the end but God's way was their beginning *praise* God.

So the lesson learned is you too can become a turn around kid also.

Just look up and ask God and he will lead you to the right way.

Jesus keep us near the cross there is one for each of us.

Sherry, Sheena, Arlene & Susan

Years apart 58
61-62-64

All that was going on back then shape them in the wrong direction.
But raised in the church they were soon realized what God had in store for them. Life back then was hard enough but to keep up was only going to get harder. So seeing what can be next was to ask God to lead them. And so they went to church sometimes and listen to the word and decided to change their route.
That rode they start was going to be long and hard.
So the turn around kids got on the right path led by God, and today life is so much better.
Praise God, thank You, Jesus.
They are now the turn around kids.

A LIFE OF A TREE

Once in a huge forest, stood a small seedling, very low down near the ground, and over him stood these very big trees; shading him with their very large umbrella-like tops . . . Keeping out the beautiful sunlight and the mist which moistened their lovely tops.

This little seedling became very depressed because it didn't seem to be growing, and it often stood in its place in a droop-like position . . . like it had no will to live. But one day, in depression, it decided to seek help, and it would raise its weak, small limbs to the other trees around it and asked, "What must I do to live?" Being so small and the trees around it so large, they didn't hear its cry for help.

So again he became discouraged, and dropped its limbs to its side. But wait . . . there was a friend to all little seedlings, someone who was probably responsible for it being in the very place where it stood. Someone so wise and so strong, who has the power to reach the lowest and the highest places anywhere around, and this friend was the Mighty Wind.

One day, when the forest was very still and quiet, the Wind blew down from above to speak to this little, troubled seedling . . . to advise him what he must do in order to grow. The Mighty Wind said, "First, you must drink enough water to strengthen your limbs, then you must raise your limbs in order to pray".

The little seedling was eager to obey, but did not understand what he had heard, and thought the Wise Wind had said to play. The little seedling did not know too much about playing either, because, first of all, he did not have any friends near him that were his size. So, he tried to talk to the birds, and the smaller animals and ask them to play with him, but they scurried about, ignoring him. He even sought the friendship of the small insects, that sometimes walked upon his tender body, but no one wanted to play with him.

So again depression set in . . . . and this time, he almost died!

Then, one day, the Mighty Wind decided to look in on his little friend, to see how he was doing . . . And when he did, he was very upset, "Oh, dear", said the Wind. "What's the matter with you?" Didn't you follow my instructions that I gave you?" The little seedling replied, "Oh yes! I tried to find someone to play with me, but no one would play with me, and I drank the water and it made my limbs strong, but then they got tired of standing up, and no one paying any attention to me . . . so here I am . . . "Oh, my poor, little friend," said the Wind, "you misunderstood me, I told you to pray, not to play; you will have plenty of time to play when you reach the top, but first you must reach this point in your life. Okay?"

"Now, listen very closely to what I am saying", said the Wind, "First, take a large drink of water to strengthen your limbs, now raise them up toward the other trees, for there you will find more strength and each day you will find yourself growing a little taller. Then you will soon receive some new food for strength . . . this is called the sunlight, and with this your body will take on a new look . . . it will grow round and green; you will be a real beauty. But you must never look down again. You must keep looking up and praying, for there is strength in prayer.

And beyond the tops of these trees, you will witness something more beautiful than you have ever seen. A beautiful blue sky, and in this sky, you will, in the daytime see the sun from which you receive your very much need strength, and also, beautiful clouds which some days turn dark to give you that much needed water to strengthen your limbs, and give your umbrella its beautiful color.

And at night, you will witness something more beautiful than you can ever imagine . . . and this is the heavens in all its glory, a clear blue sky with jewel-like forms which seem to dance and these are called stars. And there is an added attraction, which is called the moon, which, if you look closely, it seems to be smiling at you. All this that you see when you reach the top, is the welcome committee; welcoming you to a brand new life; one which will mystify you, but you will love every bit of it.

And above all these heavens, there is a God, the Ruler over us all, and the One who made you what you are. So every day, raise your leaf-laden arms in prayer. And then you can play in the breezes that I blow softly among the trees. Good-bye, my friend," said the Mighty Wind.

"Good-bye, Mighty Wind, and thank you very much", said the happy seedling.

Jeanette Curry
April 20, 11974

Autumn 10/14/11

God if I should die before I wake, please let it be in Autumn.

My favorite time of the year, to go in such splendor my soul would happily surrender.

My life on this earth was blessing. I learned a lot, I loved a lot and even laugh a lot.

Because my *father* God gave me a lot. A lot of love and wonderful people in my life who taught me a lot.

I am happy for my parents, sisters, brothers, nieces and nephews.

A great man in my late years.

Most of all four wonderful children and grands.

And added member to my life young men that are like sons to me.

I love the sunrise, the sunset, the rolling clouds and blue sky. The color of the trees and rustling from the wind.

My favorite time of year *Autumn*.

This isn't a goodbye, but a sweet surrender.

Thank You father God

I Love You

WIND/LOVE

Two four letter words = both destruction
And sometimes kind
It's amazing how these two compare not only in its
Destruction but also in its fear
It tears you up and twist you around and leave you
Lying on the ground.
Breaking up and turn around
Blowing in and out our lives
Two four letter words that's destructive and
Sometimes kind; both can be the same
They can put a smile on you or make you your mind.

Printed in the United States
By Bookmasters